WHAT'S GOIN _ _ .

90-Day Companion Journal

THIS JOURNAL BELONGS TO:

_____

_____

_____

Three Star Publishing
7327 SW Barnes Road #524
Portland, OR 97225
Tel: (503) 963-8817

Ordering information
Special discounts are available on quantity purchases. For details, contact us at (503) 963-8817 or info@gregbellspeaks.com

Printed in the United States of America

Book cover design by Catherine Veraghen of happy, inc.; gethappyinc.com
Copyediting by Sofia Joy Bell
Interior design by Jennifer Omner of ALL Publications; allpublications.com

ISBN: 978-1-935313-06-9

First Edition

Transform Your Life!

Congratulations on taking the next step to developing your *What's Going Well* mindset. This Companion Journal complements the book, *What's Going Well?: The Question That Changes Everything*, by Greg Bell. The book uncovers how the concept was developed, why it's important for your success and well-being, and gives you the foundation and tools to start embracing your own *What's Going Well* mindset. This 90-day Companion Journal will help you make the mindset a reality in your daily practice, and start experiencing all its benefits.

Here's how to use the journal:

1. First, read *What's Going Well?: The Question That Changes Everything*.

2. Throughout the book there are exercises marked with this symbol ☼. Use the space in the back of the journal to complete the exercises and write any additional thoughts and experiences you have.

3. Chapter 4 of the book, *Making What's Going Well a Habit*, challenges you to take the 90-Day *What's Going Well* Journal Challenge. Read that chapter and use this journal to capture your twice-daily *What's Going Well* thoughts, both in the morning and before going to bed. If *What's Going Well* doesn't come immediately to mind when you begin to journal, consider the things that

may be going well in the five elements that Gallup measures for determining a person's well-being,[1] plus one I've added:

- Career
- Social (relationships, both personal and professional)
- Financial (money)
- Physical (including health)
- Community
- Hobbies (my addition)

It's also helpful to think about *why* something went well. *What's Going Well* or *what went well* is often connected to a particular person, so the exercise can inform you about who you should be expressing appreciation to.

Above all, journal. Make this journal yours.

1   Rath, T. (2010). *Wellbeing: The Five Essential Elements*. Washington, DC: Gallup Press.

90 days from now you will
Thank Yourself
for starting this
What's Going Well Journey

What's Going Well? Journal Contract

I, _____, understand that I am undertaking a focused look at *What's Going Well* in my life. I commit myself to the 90-day duration. I commit to weekly reading and writing daily about *What's Going Well* in the journal upon waking and before sleeping.

Writing daily in my *What's Going Well* Journal is essential to me for the following reasons:

_____

_____

_____

I further understand that this is a journey. There will be peaks and valleys. I commit to a "media diet" and to practice self-care in the process by getting proper rest and exercise for the next 90 days.

_____

Signature

_____

Date

Date _____ / _____ / _____

"This is a wonderful day.
I've never seen this one before."
~ Maya Angelou

What's Going Well?

_____

_____

_____

_____

What Went Well?

_____

_____

_____

_____

Notes:

_____

_____

What's Going Well with:

Career   Relationships   Money   Health   Community   Hobbies

Date _____ / _____ / _____

"In ordinary life we hardly realize that
we receive a great deal more than we give,
and that it is only with gratitude that life becomes rich."
~ Dietrich Bonhoeffer

What's Going Well?

_____

_____

_____

_____

What Went Well?

_____

_____

_____

_____

Notes:

_____

_____

What's Going Well with:

Career   Relationships   Money   Health   Community   Hobbies

Date _____ / _____ / _____

"We often take for granted
the very things that most deserve our gratitude."
~ Cynthia Ozick

☀ *What's Going Well?*

_____

_____

_____

_____

☺ *What Went Well?*

_____

_____

_____

_____

Notes:

_____

_____

What's Going Well with:

Career   Relationships   Money   Health   Community   Hobbies

Date _____ / _____ / _____

*"We can choose to be grateful,
no matter what."*
~ Dieter F. Uchtdorf

What's Going Well?

_____

_____

_____

_____

What Went Well?

_____

_____

_____

_____

Notes:

_____

_____

What's Going Well with:

Career   Relationships   Money   Health   Community   Hobbies

Date _____ / _____ / _____

"Be grateful for what you already have while you pursue your goals. If you aren't grateful for what you already have, what makes you think you would be happy with more."
~ Roy T. Bennett

What's Going Well?

_____

_____

_____

_____

What Went Well?

_____

_____

_____

_____

Notes:

_____

_____

What's Going Well with:

Career   Relationships   Money   Health   Community   Hobbies

Date _____ / _____ / _____

*"We must find time to stop and thank
the people who make a difference in our lives."
~ John F. Kennedy*

☼ *What's Going Well?*

_____

_____

_____

_____

⌣ *What Went Well?*

_____

_____

_____

_____

Notes:

_____

_____

What's Going Well with:

Career   Relationships   Money   Health   Community   Hobbies

Date _____ / _____ / _____

*"When it comes to life, the critical thing is
whether you take things for granted or
take them with gratitude."*
~ G.K. Chesterton

What's Going Well?

_____

_____

_____

_____

What Went Well?

_____

_____

_____

_____

Notes:

_____

_____

What's Going Well with:

Career   Relationships   Money   Health   Community   Hobbies

What's Going Well?: The question is the answer!

Date _____ / _____ / _____

"We can complain because rose bushes have thorns,
or rejoice because thorns have roses."
~ Alphonse Karr

What's Going Well?

_____

_____

_____

_____

What Went Well?

_____

_____

_____

_____

Notes:

_____

_____

What's Going Well with:

Career   Relationships   Money   Health   Community   Hobbies

Date _____ / _____ / _____

*"I would maintain that thanks are the highest form of thought,
and that gratitude is happiness doubled by wonder."*
~ Gilbert K. Chesterton

☀ *What's Going Well?*

_____

_____

_____

_____

What Went Well?

_____

_____

_____

_____

Notes:

_____

_____

What's Going Well with:

Career   Relationships   Money   Health   Community   Hobbies

Date _____ / _____ / _____

"I was complaining that I had no shoes
till I met a man who had no feet."
~ Confucius

What's Going Well?

_____

_____

_____

_____

What Went Well?

_____

_____

_____

_____

Notes:

_____

_____

What's Going Well with:

Career   Relationships   Money   Health   Community   Hobbies

Date _____ / _____ / _____

"Gratitude is riches. Complaint is poverty."
~ Doris Day

☀ *What's Going Well?*

_____

_____

_____

_____

⌣ *What Went Well?*

_____

_____

_____

_____

Notes:

_____

_____

What's Going Well with:

Career   Relationships   Money   Health   Community   Hobbies

Date _____ / _____ / _____

"So much has been given to me;
I have no time to ponder over that which has been denied."
~ Helen Keller

What's Going Well?

_____

_____

_____

_____

What Went Well?

_____

_____

_____

_____

Notes:

_____

_____

What's Going Well with:

Career   Relationships   Money   Health   Community   Hobbies

Date _____ / _____ / _____

"Stop now. Enjoy the moment. It's now or never."
~ Maxime Lagacé

☀ *What's Going Well?*

_____

_____

_____

_____

What Went Well?

_____

_____

_____

_____

Notes:

_____

_____

What's Going Well with:

Career   Relationships   Money   Health   Community   Hobbies

Date _____ / _____ / _____

"There are only two ways to live your life.
One is as though nothing is a miracle.
The other is as though everything is a miracle."
~ Albert Einstein

What's Going Well?

_____

_____

_____

_____

What Went Well?

_____

_____

_____

_____

Notes:

_____

_____

What's Going Well with:

Career   Relationships   Money   Health   Community   Hobbies

Start the day with gratitude

~~~~~~~~~~~~~~~~~~~~~~~~~~~~

Date _____ / _____ / _____

"Gratitude is not only the greatest of virtues,
but the parent of all others."
~ Marcus Tullius Ciceroy

What's Going Well?

_____

_____

_____

_____

What Went Well?

_____

_____

_____

_____

Notes:

_____

_____

What's Going Well with:

Career   Relationships   Money   Health   Community   Hobbies

Date _____ / _____ / _____

"The essence of all beautiful art is gratitude."
~ Friedrich Nietzche

☀ *What's Going Well?*

_____

_____

_____

_____

⌣ *What Went Well?*

_____

_____

_____

_____

Notes:

_____

_____

What's Going Well with:

Career   Relationships   Money   Health   Community   Hobbies

Date _____ / _____ / _____

*"The deepest craving of human nature is
the need to be appreciated."*
~ William James

☀ *What's Going Well?*

_____

_____

_____

_____

⌣ *What Went Well?*

_____

_____

_____

_____

Notes:

_____

_____

What's Going Well with:

Career   Relationships   Money   Health   Community   Hobbies

Date _____ / _____ / _____

"Gratitude is the fairest blossom that springs from the soul."
~ Henry Ward Beecher

What's Going Well?

_____

_____

_____

_____

What Went Well?

_____

_____

_____

_____

Notes:

_____

_____

What's Going Well with:

Career   Relationships   Money   Health   Community   Hobbies

Date _____ / _____ / _____

"Ingratitude is monstrous."
~ William Shakespeare

What's Going Well?

_____

_____

_____

_____

What Went Well?

_____

_____

_____

_____

Notes:

_____

_____

What's Going Well with:

Career   Relationships   Money   Health   Community   Hobbies

Date _____ / _____ / _____

"The best way to pay for a lovely moment is to enjoy it."
~ Richard Bach

What's Going Well?

_____

_____

_____

_____

What Went Well?

_____

_____

_____

_____

Notes:

_____

_____

What's Going Well with:

Career   Relationships   Money   Health   Community   Hobbies

Date _____ / _____ / _____

"Nothing is more honorable than a grateful heart."
~ Lucius Annaeus Seneca

☀ *What's Going Well?*

_____

_____

_____

_____

What Went Well?

_____

_____

_____

_____

Notes:

_____

_____

What's Going Well with:

Career   Relationships   Money   Health   Community   Hobbies

Choose
gratitude

~~~~~~~~~~~~~~~~~~~~~~~~~~~~~~~~~~~~~~

Date _____ / _____ / _____

"What separates privilege from entitlement is gratitude."
~ Brené Brown

What's Going Well?

_____

_____

_____

_____

What Went Well?

_____

_____

_____

_____

Notes:

_____

_____

What's Going Well with:

Career   Relationships   Money   Health   Community   Hobbies

Date _____ / _____ / _____

"Gratitude turns what we have into enough."
~ Aesop

What's Going Well?

_____

_____

_____

_____

What Went Well?

_____

_____

_____

_____

Notes:

_____

_____

What's Going Well with:

Career   Relationships   Money   Health   Community   Hobbies

Date _____ / _____ / _____

"There are always flowers for those who want to see them."
~ Henri Matisse

☀ *What's Going Well?*

_____

_____

_____

_____

⌣ *What Went Well?*

_____

_____

_____

_____

Notes:

_____

_____

What's Going Well with:

Career   Relationships   Money   Health   Community   Hobbies

Date _____ / _____ / _____

"Every blessing ignored becomes a curse."
~ Paulo Coelho

☀ *What's Going Well?*

_____

_____

_____

_____

What Went Well?

_____

_____

_____

_____

Notes:

_____

_____

What's Going Well with:

Career   Relationships   Money   Health   Community   Hobbies

Date _____ / _____ / _____

"Find the good and praise it."
~ Alex Haley

☼ *What's Going Well?*

_____

_____

_____

_____

⌣ *What Went Well?*

_____

_____

_____

_____

Notes:

_____

_____

What's Going Well with:

Career   Relationships   Money   Health   Community   Hobbies

Date _____ / _____ / _____

"Gratitude unlocks the fullness of life."
~ Melody Beattie

☼ *What's Going Well?*

_____

_____

_____

_____

⌣ *What Went Well?*

_____

_____

_____

_____

Notes:

_____

_____

What's Going Well with:

Career   Relationships   Money   Health   Community   Hobbies

Date _____ / _____ / _____

"Gratitude and attitude are not challenges; they are choices."
~ Robert Braathe

What's Going Well?

_____

_____

_____

_____

What Went Well?

_____

_____

_____

_____

Notes:

_____

_____

What's Going Well with:

Career   Relationships   Money   Health   Community   Hobbies

Begin each day with a grateful heart

Date _____ / _____ / _____

"If you count all your assets, you always show a profit."
~ Robert Quillen

☀ *What's Going Well?*

_____

_____

_____

_____

⌣ *What Went Well?*

_____

_____

_____

_____

Notes:

_____

_____

What's Going Well with:
Career   Relationships   Money   Health   Community   Hobbies

Date _____ / _____ / _____

*"If you don't appreciate what you have,
you may as well not have it."
~ Rosalene Glickman*

What's Going Well?

_____

_____

_____

_____

What Went Well?

_____

_____

_____

_____

Notes:

_____

_____

What's Going Well with:

Career   Relationships   Money   Health   Community   Hobbies

Date _____ / _____ / _____

*"Do not spoil what you have by
desiring what you have not."*
~ Epicurus

What's Going Well?

_____

_____

_____

_____

What Went Well?

_____

_____

_____

_____

Notes:

_____

_____

What's Going Well with:

Career   Relationships   Money   Health   Community   Hobbies

Date _____ / _____ / _____

"When life is sweet, say thank you and celebrate.
And when life is bitter, say thank you and grow."
~ Shauna Niequist

What's Going Well?

_____

_____

_____

_____

What Went Well?

_____

_____

_____

_____

Notes:

_____

_____

What's Going Well with:

Career   Relationships   Money   Health   Community   Hobbies

Date _____ / _____ / _____

*"You won't be happy with more
until you're happy with what you've got."
~ Viki King*

What's Going Well?

_____

_____

_____

_____

What Went Well?

_____

_____

_____

_____

Notes:

_____

_____

What's Going Well with:

Career   Relationships   Money   Health   Community   Hobbies

Date _____ / _____ / _____

"Appreciation is a wonderful thing.
It makes what is excellent in others belong to us as well."
~ Voltaire

☀ *What's Going Well?*

_____

_____

_____

_____

What Went Well?

_____

_____

_____

_____

Notes:

_____

_____

What's Going Well with:

Career   Relationships   Money   Health   Community   Hobbies

Date _____ / _____ / _____

"The thankful receiver bears a plentiful harvest."
~ William Blake

☀ *What's Going Well?*

_____

_____

_____

_____

⌣ *What Went Well?*

_____

_____

_____

_____

Notes:

_____

_____

What's Going Well with:

Career   Relationships   Money   Health   Community   Hobbies

Cultivate the habit of being grateful

Date _____ / _____ / _____

"There's no disaster that can't become a blessing,
and no blessing that can't become a disaster."
~ Richard Bach

What's Going Well?

_____

_____

_____

_____

What Went Well?

_____

_____

_____

_____

Notes:

_____

_____

What's Going Well with:

Career   Relationships   Money   Health   Community   Hobbies

Date _____ / _____ / _____

"Train yourself never to put off the
word or action for the expression of gratitude."
~ Albert Schweitzer

What's Going Well?

_____

_____

_____

_____

What Went Well?

_____

_____

_____

_____

Notes:

_____

_____

What's Going Well with:
Career   Relationships   Money   Health   Community   Hobbies

Date _____ / _____ / _____

"Gratitude can turn a meal into a feast."
~ Melody Beattie

☼ *What's Going Well?*

_____

_____

_____

_____

◡ *What Went Well?*

_____

_____

_____

_____

Notes:

_____

_____

What's Going Well with:

Career   Relationships   Money   Health   Community   Hobbies

Date _____ / _____ / _____

*"The hardest arithmetic to master is
that which enables us to count our blessings."
~ Eric Hoffer*

What's Going Well?

_____

_____

_____

_____

What Went Well?

_____

_____

_____

_____

Notes:

_____

_____

What's Going Well with:

Career   Relationships   Money   Health   Community   Hobbies

Date _____ / _____ / _____

"Joy is a heart full and a mind purified by gratitude."
~ Marietta McCarty

☀ *What's Going Well?*

_____

_____

_____

_____

What Went Well?

_____

_____

_____

_____

Notes:

_____

_____

What's Going Well with:

Career   Relationships   Money   Health   Community   Hobbies

Date _____ / _____ / _____

"If you want to find happiness, find gratitude."
~ Steve Maraboli

☀ *What's Going Well?*

_____

_____

_____

_____

🙂 *What Went Well?*

_____

_____

_____

_____

Notes:

_____

_____

What's Going Well with:

Career   Relationships   Money   Health   Community   Hobbies

Date _____ / _____ / _____

"Gratitude is one of the sweet shortcuts to finding peace of mind and happiness inside. No matter what is going on outside of us, there's always something we could be grateful for."
~ Barry Neil Kaufman

What's Going Well?

_____

_____

_____

_____

What Went Well?

_____

_____

_____

_____

Notes:

_____

_____

What's Going Well with:

Career   Relationships   Money   Health   Community   Hobbies

Appreciation can change a day

Date _____ / _____ / _____

"The way to move out of judgment is to move into gratitude."
~ Neale Donald Walsch

What's Going Well?

_____

_____

_____

_____

What Went Well?

_____

_____

_____

_____

Notes:

_____

_____

What's Going Well with:

Career   Relationships   Money   Health   Community   Hobbies

Date _____ / _____ / _____

"Gratitude helps you to grow and expand;
gratitude brings joy and laughter into your life
and into the lives of all those around you."
~ Eileen Caddy

What's Going Well?

_____

_____

_____

_____

What Went Well?

_____

_____

_____

_____

Notes:

_____

_____

What's Going Well with:

Career   Relationships   Money   Health   Community   Hobbies

Date ——— / ——— / ———

"Through the eyes of gratitude, everything is a miracle."
~ Mary Davis

What's Going Well?

_____

_____

_____

_____

What Went Well?

_____

_____

_____

_____

Notes:

_____

_____

What's Going Well with:

Career   Relationships   Money   Health   Community   Hobbies

Date ____ / ____ / ____

*"It is impossible to feel grateful
and depressed in the same moment."*
~ Naomi Williams

☀ *What's Going Well?*

_____

_____

_____

_____

‿ *What Went Well?*

_____

_____

_____

_____

Notes:

_____

_____

What's Going Well with:

Career   Relationships   Money   Health   Community   Hobbies

Date ——— / ——— / ———

*"The only people with whom you should try to get even
are those who have helped you."*
~ John E. Southard

What's Going Well?

_____

_____

_____

_____

What Went Well?

_____

_____

_____

_____

Notes:

_____

_____

What's Going Well with:

Career   Relationships   Money   Health   Community   Hobbies

Date _____ / _____ / _____

*"Think with great gratitude of those
who have lighted the flame within us."*
~ Albert Schweitzer

What's Going Well?

_____

_____

_____

_____

What Went Well?

_____

_____

_____

_____

Notes:

_____

_____

What's Going Well with:

Career   Relationships   Money   Health   Community   Hobbies

Date _____ / _____ / _____

"The most important thing is to enjoy your life—
to be happy—it's all that matters."
~ Audrey Hepburn

What's Going Well?

_____

_____

_____

_____

What Went Well?

_____

_____

_____

_____

Notes:

_____

_____

What's Going Well with:

Career   Relationships   Money   Health   Community   Hobbies

Gratitude
is the best
attitude

~~~~~~~~~~~~~~~~~~~~~~~~~~~~~~~~

Date _____ / _____ / _____

*"We should certainly count our blessings,
but we should also make our blessings count."*
~ Neal A. Maxwell

What's Going Well?

_____

_____

_____

_____

What Went Well?

_____

_____

_____

_____

Notes:

_____

_____

What's Going Well with:

Career   Relationships   Money   Health   Community   Hobbies

Date _____ / _____ / _____

"Embrace your life journey with gratitude,
so that how you travel your path is more important
than reaching your ultimate destination."
~ Rosalene Glickman

☀ *What's Going Well?*

_____

_____

_____

_____

What Went Well?

_____

_____

_____

_____

Notes:

_____

_____

What's Going Well with:

Career   Relationships   Money   Health   Community   Hobbies

Date _____ / _____ / _____

*"The more you recognize and
express gratitude for the things you have,
the more things you will have to express gratitude for."*
~ Zig Ziglar

What's Going Well?

_____

_____

_____

_____

What Went Well?

_____

_____

_____

_____

Notes:

_____

_____

What's Going Well with:

Career   Relationships   Money   Health   Community   Hobbies

Date _____ / _____ / _____

"In order to attract more of the blessings that life has to offer,
you must truly appreciate what you already have."
~ Ralph Marston

What's Going Well?

_____

_____

_____

_____

What Went Well?

_____

_____

_____

_____

Notes:

_____

_____

What's Going Well with:

Career   Relationships   Money   Health   Community   Hobbies

Date _____ / _____ / _____

*"Enjoy the little things for one day you may look back
and realize they were the big things."*
~ Robert Brault

What's Going Well?

_____

_____

_____

_____

What Went Well?

_____

_____

_____

_____

Notes:

_____

_____

What's Going Well with:

Career   Relationships   Money   Health   Community   Hobbies

Date ＿＿ / ＿＿ / ＿＿

"Appreciation can make a day, even change a life.
Your willingness to put it into words is all that is necessary."
~ Margaret Cousins

What's Going Well?

_____

_____

_____

_____

What Went Well?

_____

_____

_____

_____

Notes:

_____

_____

What's Going Well with:

Career   Relationships   Money   Health   Community   Hobbies

Date _____ / _____ / _____

*"Feeling grateful or appreciative of someone or
something in your life actually attracts more of the things
that you appreciate and value into your life."*
~ Christiane Northrup

What's Going Well?

_____

_____

_____

_____

What Went Well?

_____

_____

_____

_____

Notes:

_____

_____

What's Going Well with:

Career   Relationships   Money   Health   Community   Hobbies

If worry
worked, there
would be no
problems

~~~~~~~~~~~~~~~~~~~~~~~~~~~~~~~

Date _____ / _____ / _____

*"Whatever you appreciate and
give thanks for will increase in your life."*
~ Sanaya Roman

What's Going Well?

_____

_____

_____

_____

What Went Well?

_____

_____

_____

_____

Notes:

_____

_____

What's Going Well with:

Career   Relationships   Money   Health   Community   Hobbies

Date _____ / _____ / _____

*"What seems to us as bitter trials
are often blessings in disguise."*
~ Oscar Wilde

What's Going Well?

_____

_____

_____

_____

What Went Well?

_____

_____

_____

_____

Notes:

_____

_____

What's Going Well with:

Career   Relationships   Money   Health   Community   Hobbies

Date _____ / _____ / _____

*"Gratitude makes sense of our past, brings peace for today,
and creates a vision for tomorrow."*
~ Melody Beattie

What's Going Well?

_____

_____

_____

_____

What Went Well?

_____

_____

_____

_____

Notes:

_____

_____

What's Going Well with:

Career   Relationships   Money   Health   Community   Hobbies

Date _____ / _____ / _____

"When I started counting my blessings,
my whole life turned around."
~ Willie Nelson

What's Going Well?

_____

_____

_____

_____

What Went Well?

_____

_____

_____

_____

Notes:

_____

_____

What's Going Well with:

Career   Relationships   Money   Health   Community   Hobbies

Date _____ / _____ / _____

*"I am happy because I'm grateful. I choose to be grateful.
That gratitude allows me to be happy."*
~ Will Arnett

What's Going Well?

_____

_____

_____

_____

What Went Well?

_____

_____

_____

_____

Notes:

_____

_____

What's Going Well with:

Career   Relationships   Money   Health   Community   Hobbies

Date _____ / _____ / _____

*"No one who achieves success does so without the help of others.
The wise and confident acknowledge this help with gratitude."*
~ Alfred North Whitehead

What's Going Well?

_____

_____

_____

_____

What Went Well?

_____

_____

_____

_____

Notes:

_____

_____

What's Going Well with:

Career   Relationships   Money   Health   Community   Hobbies

Date _____ / _____ / _____

"I may not be where I want to be but
I'm thankful for not being where I used to be."
~ Habeeb Akande

What's Going Well?

_____

_____

_____

_____

What Went Well?

_____

_____

_____

_____

Notes:

_____

_____

What's Going Well with:

Career   Relationships   Money   Health   Community   Hobbies

Gratitude works

~~~~~~~~~~~~~~~~~~~~~~~~~~~~~~~~~~

Date _____ / _____ / _____

*"Be grateful for what you have,
work hard for what you don't have."*
~ Unknown

☀ *What's Going Well?*

_____

_____

_____

_____

What Went Well?

_____

_____

_____

_____

Notes:

_____

_____

What's Going Well with:

Career   Relationships   Money   Health   Community   Hobbies

Date _____ / _____ / _____

ou are gracious, you have won the game."
~ Stevie Nicks

What's Going Well?

_____

_____

_____

_____

What Went Well?

_____

_____

_____

_____

Notes:

_____

_____

What's Going Well with:

Career   Relationships   Money   Health   Community   Hobbies

Date _____ / _____ / _____

"Give thanks for a little and you will find a lot."
~ Hansa Proverb

What's Going Well?

_____

_____

_____

_____

What Went Well?

_____

_____

_____

_____

Notes:

_____

_____

What's Going Well with:

Career   Relationships   Money   Health   Community   Hobbies

Date _____ / _____ / _____

*"Gratitude is the ability to experience life as a gift.
It liberates us from the prison of self-preoccupation."*
~ John Ortberg

What's Going Well?

_____

_____

_____

_____

What Went Well?

_____

_____

_____

_____

Notes:

_____

_____

What's Going Well with:

Career   Relationships   Money   Health   Community   Hobbies

Date ———— / ———— / ————

*"Learn to be thankful for what you already have,
while you pursue all that you want."*
~ Lydia Sweatt

What's Going Well?

_____

_____

_____

_____

What Went Well?

_____

_____

_____

_____

Notes:

_____

_____

What's Going Well with:

Career   Relationships   Money   Health   Community   Hobbies

Date _____ / _____ / _____

"The way to develop the best that is in a person
is by appreciation and encouragement."
~ Charles Schwab

☀ *What's Going Well?*

_____

_____

_____

_____

What Went Well?

_____

_____

_____

_____

Notes:

_____

_____

What's Going Well with:

Career   Relationships   Money   Health   Community   Hobbies

Date _____ / _____ / _____

*"One way to love yourself and take charge of your life
is through the practice of gratitude.
Practicing gratitude increases self-awareness."*
~ *Veronica Smith*

What's Going Well?

_____

_____

_____

_____

What Went Well?

_____

_____

_____

_____

Notes:

_____

_____

What's Going Well with:
Career   Relationships   Money   Health   Community   Hobbies

Expect
nothing.
Appreciate
everything.

~~~~~~~~~~~~~~~~~~~~~~~~~~~~~~~~~

Date _____ / _____ / _____

"Appreciate what you have, where you are and who you are with in this moment."
~ Tony Clark

What's Going Well?

_____

_____

_____

_____

What Went Well?

_____

_____

_____

_____

Notes:

_____

_____

What's Going Well with:

Career   Relationships   Money   Health   Community   Hobbies

Date _____ / _____ / _____

"Whenever I count my blessings, I find myself becoming more grateful because the good things of life outweigh the not so pleasant things that are happening in my life."
~ James Jason

What's Going Well?

_____

_____

_____

_____

What Went Well?

_____

_____

_____

_____

Notes:

_____

_____

What's Going Well with:

Career   Relationships   Money   Health   Community   Hobbies

Date _____ / _____ / _____

"Be verbal in acknowledging your appreciation."
~ Catherine Pulsifer

What's Going Well?

_____

_____

_____

_____

What Went Well?

_____

_____

_____

_____

Notes:

_____

_____

What's Going Well with:

Career   Relationships   Money   Health   Community   Hobbies

Date ____ / ____ / ____

"Life holds so many simple blessings,
each day bringing its own individual wonder.""
~ John McLeod

☀ *What's Going Well?*

_____

_____

_____

_____

What Went Well?

_____

_____

_____

_____

Notes:

_____

_____

What's Going Well with:
Career   Relationships   Money   Health   Community   Hobbies

Date _____ / _____ / _____

*"One way to combat the gloom is to wake up each day and reflect
on what you are grateful for. You can find at least
one thing to appreciate each day."*
~ Carla Loving

What's Going Well?

_____

_____

_____

_____

What Went Well?

_____

_____

_____

_____

Notes:

_____

_____

What's Going Well with:

Career   Relationships   Money   Health   Community   Hobbies

Date _____ / _____ / _____

"Think of a special friend or person you admire. Think of the love and appreciation you have for them. Think of the qualities that make them stand out for you."
~ Jenny Clift

What's Going Well?

_____

_____

_____

_____

What Went Well?

_____

_____

_____

_____

Notes:

_____

_____

What's Going Well with:

Career   Relationships   Money   Health   Community   Hobbies

Date _____ / _____ / _____

*"Instead of being impatient because you have to
wait for something, be grateful for the extra time you have now
to notice and appreciate your surroundings."*
~ Danielle Tinning

What's Going Well?

_____

_____

_____

_____

What Went Well?

_____

_____

_____

_____

Notes:

_____

_____

What's Going Well with:

Career   Relationships   Money   Health   Community   Hobbies

Focus on
the good

Date _____ / _____ / _____

*"A grateful mind is a great mind which
eventually attracts to itself great things."*
~ Plato

What's Going Well?

_____

_____

_____

_____

What Went Well?

_____

_____

_____

_____

Notes:

_____

_____

What's Going Well with:

Career   Relationships   Money   Health   Community   Hobbies

Date _____ / _____ / _____

*"I don't have to chase extraordinary moments to find happiness—
it's right in front of me if I am paying attention
and practicing gratitude."*
~ Brené Brown

What's Going Well?

_____

_____

_____

_____

What Went Well?

_____

_____

_____

_____

Notes:

_____

_____

What's Going Well with:

Career   Relationships   Money   Health   Community   Hobbies

Date _____ / _____ / _____

*"Developing an 'attitude of gratitude' is one of
the simplest ways to improve your satisfaction with life."*
~ Amy Morin

What's Going Well?

_____

_____

_____

_____

What Went Well?

_____

_____

_____

_____

Notes:

_____

_____

What's Going Well with:
Career   Relationships   Money   Health   Community   Hobbies

Date _____ / _____ / _____

"Gratitude should not be just a reaction to getting what you want, but an all-the-time gratitude, the kind where you notice the little things and where you constantly look for the good, even in unpleasant situations."
~ Marelisa Fabrega

What's Going Well?

_____

_____

_____

_____

What Went Well?

_____

_____

_____

_____

Notes:

_____

_____

What's Going Well with:

Career   Relationships   Money   Health   Community   Hobbies

Date _____ / _____ / _____

"Maybe the simplest and most effortless habit for living a happier life is to take one or a few minutes every day to focus on what is already here and that you can be grateful for in your life."
~ Henrik Edberg

What's Going Well?

_____

_____

_____

_____

What Went Well?

_____

_____

_____

_____

Notes:

_____

_____

What's Going Well with:

Career   Relationships   Money   Health   Community   Hobbies

Date _____ / _____ / _____

*"Gratitude leads to greatness. It can literally turn
what you have into more than enough, jobs into joy,
chaos into order, uncertainty into clarity, and
bring peace to an otherwise chaotic day."*
~ Marc Chernoff

What's Going Well?

_____

_____

_____

_____

What Went Well?

_____

_____

_____

_____

Notes:

_____

_____

What's Going Well with:

Career   Relationships   Money   Health   Community   Hobbies

Date _____ / _____ / _____

"Gratitude is an antidote to negative emotions, a neutralizer of envy, hostility, worry, and irritation. It is savoring; it is not taking things for granted; it is present oriented."
~ Sonja Lyubomirskyy

What's Going Well?

_____

_____

_____

_____

What Went Well?

_____

_____

_____

_____

Notes:

_____

_____

What's Going Well with:

Career   Relationships   Money   Health   Community   Hobbies

Savor the
little things

~~~~~~~~~~~~~~~~~~~~~

Date _____ / _____ / _____

"Piglet noticed that even though he had a Very Small Heart,
it could hold a rather large amount of Gratitude."
~ A.A. Milne, Winnie-The-Pooh

What's Going Well?

_____

_____

_____

_____

What Went Well?

_____

_____

_____

_____

Notes:

_____

_____

What's Going Well with:

Career   Relationships   Money   Health   Community   Hobbies

Date _____ / _____ / _____

*"Opening your eyes to more of the world around you
can deeply enhance your gratitude practice."*
~ Derrick Carpenter

What's Going Well?

_____

_____

_____

_____

What Went Well?

_____

_____

_____

_____

Notes:

_____

_____

What's Going Well with:

Career   Relationships   Money   Health   Community   Hobbies

Date _____ / _____ / _____

"Summoning gratitude is a sure way to get our life back on track. Opening our eyes to affirm gratitude grows the garden of our inner abundance, just as standing close to a fire eventually warms our heart."
~ Alexandra Katehakis

What's Going Well?

_____

_____

_____

_____

What Went Well?

_____

_____

_____

_____

Notes:

_____

_____

What's Going Well with:

Career   Relationships   Money   Health   Community   Hobbies

Date _____ / _____ / _____

"Not having the best situation, but seeing the best in your situation is the key to happiness."
~ Marie Forleo

What's Going Well?

_____

_____

_____

_____

What Went Well?

_____

_____

_____

_____

Notes:

_____

_____

What's Going Well with:

Career   Relationships   Money   Health   Community   Hobbies

Date _____ / _____ / _____

*"When you focus on gratitude, positive things flow in
more readily, making you even more grateful."*
~ Lissa Rankin

What's Going Well?

_____

_____

_____

_____

What Went Well?

_____

_____

_____

_____

Notes:

_____

_____

What's Going Well with:

Career   Relationships   Money   Health   Community   Hobbies

Date _____ / _____ / _____

"Gratitude goes beyond good manners—
it's a mindset and a lifestyle."
~ Andrea Reiser

What's Going Well?

_____

_____

_____

_____

What Went Well?

_____

_____

_____

_____

Notes:

_____

_____

What's Going Well with:
Career   Relationships   Money   Health   Community   Hobbies

CONGRATULATIONS!

You just finished 90 days of the *What's Going Well* journey

Take some time and reflect on your journey. Read through some of your entries. Take inventory on how you feel and what you think now compared to when you started the journey. How has the *What's Going Well* mindset changed your life?

Be sure to get a new copy of the Journal so you can continue the journey.

Additional Resources

Subscribe to the *What's Going Well* journey emails
The *What's Going Well* journey emails provide you with ongoing reminders to reflect on *What's Going Well* in your life. The emails are a perfect companion to the book and 90-day journal—gregbellspeaks.com/wgw

Download the *What's Going Well for Teams Guide*
This free guide provides a 10-step process for incorporating the *What's Going Well* principles into your organization—gregbellspeaks.com/wgw-leaders-guide

See Greg Bell's Recommended Reading List
For Greg Bell's recommended reading list, go to gregbellspeaks.com/reading-list

Note Pages
for Exercises from
the book,
What's Going Well?
The question that changes everything.

"A moment of gratitude makes a difference in your attitude."
~ Bruce Wilkinson

_____

_____

_____

_____

_____

_____

_____

_____

_____

_____

_____

_____

_____

"Having problems at work? Be grateful you have work. Be grateful you have challenges, and that life isn't boring. Be grateful that you can learn from these challenges. Be thankful they make you a stronger person."

~ Leo Babauta

"The more gratitude practice you perform in daily life, the deeper the benefits go and the more profound and life-altering the benefits truly are."
~ Carla Clark

_____

_____

_____

_____

_____

_____

_____

_____

_____

_____

_____

_____

_____

_____

"Acknowledging the good that you already have in your life is the foundation for all abundance."
~ Eckhart Tolle

_____

_____

_____

_____

_____

_____

_____

_____

_____

_____

_____

_____

_____

_____

_____

_____

"Gratitude is gentle reminder to recognize the sweet privilege of health, hope and heartbeat over the need for 'stuff'."

~ Kristin Granger

_____

_____

_____

_____

_____

_____

_____

_____

_____

_____

_____

_____

_____

_____

The real gift of gratitude is that the more grateful you are,
the more present you become."
~ Robert Holden

_____

_____

_____

_____

_____

_____

_____

_____

_____

_____

_____

_____

_____

_____

_____

_____

"You will never have enough, do enough or be enough, until you see yourself today as enough."

~ Cindy Keating

_____

_____

_____

_____

_____

_____

_____

_____

_____

_____

_____

_____

_____

_____

"If you want to find happiness, find gratitude."
~ Steve Maraboli

_____

_____

_____

_____

_____

_____

_____

_____

_____

_____

_____

_____

_____

_____

_____

_____

"Gratitude always comes into play; research shows that people are happier if they are grateful for the positive things in their lives, rather than worrying about what might be missing."

~ Dan Buettner

_____

_____

_____

_____

_____

_____

_____

_____

_____

_____

_____

_____

_____

_____

_____

_____

"Gratitude is a powerful catalyst for happiness.
It's the spark that lights a fire of joy in your soul."
~ Amy Collette

_____

_____

_____

_____

_____

_____

_____

_____

_____

_____

_____

_____

_____

_____

_____

_____

*"I looked around and thought about my life. I felt grateful.
I noticed every detail. That is the key to time travel.
You can only move if you are actually in the moment.
You have to be where you are to get where you need to go."*
~ Amy Poehler

"It's up to us to choose contentment and thankfulness now—
and to stop imagining that we have to
have everything perfect before we'll be happy."
~ Joanna Gaines

_____

_____

_____

_____

_____

_____

_____

_____

_____

_____

_____

_____

_____

_____

_____

_____

"Life is both beautiful and painful. In whatever situation we find ourselves in, no matter how unfortunate it may seem, there is always something to be thankful for— if we only choose to see it."

~ *Frederick Espiritu*

_____

_____

_____

_____

_____

_____

_____

_____

_____

_____

_____

_____

_____

_____

"Gratitude is a currency that we can mint for ourselves, and spend without fear of bankruptcy."

~ Fred De Witt Van Amburgh

_____

_____

_____

_____

_____

_____

_____

_____

_____

_____

_____

_____

_____

_____

"Dance. Smile. Giggle. Marvel. TRUST. HOPE. LOVE. WISH. BELIEVE. Most of all, enjoy every moment of the journey, and appreciate where you are at this moment instead of always focusing on how far you have to go."

~ Mandy Hale

"Being thankful is not always experienced as a natural state of existence, we must work at it, akin to a type of strength training for the heart."
~ Larissa Gomes

_____

_____

_____

_____

_____

_____

_____

_____

_____

_____

_____

_____

_____

_____

About the Author

Greg Bell

Greg Bell is an author, motivational speaker, thought leader, and business consultant. He has inspired an array of organizations, from Fortune 500 companies like Nike, Disney, and Comcast, to athletic teams like the Portland Trailblazers, Oregon Ducks Football, and Gonzaga Bulldogs Basketball.

As an innovator and keen observer of highly successful leaders and teams, Greg has learned that the key to success is having the courage to use the skills you already have to achieve a result greater than you previously imagined.

Inspiring and energizing audiences with his engaging storytelling, Greg shares his knowledge with excitement and passion. His ability to masterfully blend insight and encouragement with just the right dose of reality makes him the consistently top-rated keynote speaker at major conferences. A Certified Speaking Professional (the highest earned designation from the National Speakers Association), Greg influences thousands of individuals and teams each year with his innate ability to connect personally with audience members.

Whether you're rolling out a new culture initiative, developing your leaders, or seeking a keynote that will be remembered long after your event, Greg will deliver a tailored session that will encourage and inspire each attendee to become stronger, more empowered, and more productive than ever before.

Greg holds political science and law degrees from the University of Oregon, where he played Division I basketball and was consistently named Most Inspirational Player. He is also the force behind Coaches vs. Cancer—a campaign for the American Cancer Society that has raised over $100 million for cancer research. In addition to his corporate leadership experience, Bell is a TEDx Talk alum, serves on the advisory board for the Portland TEDx conference series, and is a Trustee for the University of Oregon Foundation.

Greg lives in Portland, Oregon with his wife Claire and has three daughters, whose middle names are Grace, Hope and Joy.

Greg Bell Seminars

To learn more about Greg's keynotes and leadership seminars, or to book Greg for your event, visit gregbellspeaks.com or call 1-877-833-3552. Greg looks forward to customizing a program for your next event!

Ordering Information

To buy multiple copies of this book or journals for your team, go to gregbellspeaks.com/books.

Stay Connected

Sign Up for Greg Bell's Newsletter
Receive helpful reminders and tips. Sign up at gregbellspeaks.com

Attend a Seminar
If you want to be the best at what you do, join Greg at a public seminar. Learn more and register at gregbellspeaks.com

Follow Greg on Social Media

 @gregbellspeaks

 @gregbellspeaks

 @gregbellspeaks

Get More Information and Visit the Website
For extra content, support, guides, or to contact us, visit gregbellspeaks.com

CPSIA information can be obtained
at www.ICGtesting.com
Printed in the USA
BVHW071501291118
534236BV00007B/22/P

9 781935 313069